Daddy Day, Daughter Day

By Larry King
and Chaia King

Illustrated by
Wendy Christensen

DOVE KIDS

Thanks to Stacy Woolf—daughter of my late agent and friend Bob Woolf—
who is going to be a major name in the world of book agentry,
and who was a major factor in making this project work.
L.K.

ISBN: 0-7871-0490-6

Printed in the USA

A Dove Kids Book
A Division of Dove Entertainment
8955 Beverly Boulevard
Los Angeles, CA 90048

Distributed by Penguin USA

Cover design by Rick Penn-Kraus

Type design by Carolyn Wendt

First printing: April 1997

10 9 8 7 6 5 4 3

I am standing at the window waiting.
Waiting for Daddy.

Chaia's mommy and I are divorced.
It's not easy being divorced.

I remember how Daddy used to carry me
outside at night to look at the stars in the
southern sky. He would sing "When You Wish
Upon a Star," and then I would ask him to tell
me a prince story.

*It's not easy being a daddy when
you don't live with a daughter you
love very much. But I talk to my
daughter Chaia every day.*

My dog, Bram, always warns me
when Daddy is a block away.
Daddy never understands how
I always manage to be waiting
outside when he arrives.

*Usually once a week I get to pick Chaia up
and spend the whole day with her. I go to bed
early the night before because I know I'm
getting up to have a day with my daughter.*

My parents have been divorced for five years, and it is still hard. I feel like I don't have a complete family. But Daddy visits often, and Mommy is happy for us to have time together. We are going on an adventure today. Daddy has lots of things planned.

I get into my car real early in the morning. I know she loves this car. It's a convertible. I put the top down and I zip over to my daughter's house.

On a day with Daddy, I kiss my mom good-bye and run to my father's dark brown Cougar with the tan color inside. It's a big car, and Daddy's leather boots shine as we drive along. We have a secret. Daddy lets me steer the car from the center of the seat. He always makes me feel grown-up and special.

There's a brief hello to her mother—just brief—and then little Chaia is in the car, and the thrilling day begins. We always go to her favorite place. She doesn't tell any of her friends about it. She doesn't tell her mother about it. Maybe her dog knows, but I doubt it.

The first place Daddy takes me to is our secret park. Only my daddy and I know where this park is. It has a magical feeling to it, like being in the wilderness. We live in Florida, where it is almost always sunny and the clouds are beautiful. Fruit trees and flowers grow everywhere.

Chaia gets to play among all the things she likes so much—her special things in her secret place. When she's finished playing, she always comes over to me and gives me a little hug and says, "This will always be our special place."

I play on the swings for a while, and then Daddy says it is time for lunch.

Lunch is always Burger King® because Chaia loves it there. If we're going out to eat, that's her favorite place.

I have a Whopper® and fries, and Daddy asks me how I am doing. I tell him how much I miss him and how lonely the house is without both of my parents there. Daddy tells me things happen in life that aren't always good—like divorce. He says it wasn't my fault and that both he and my mommy love me very much.

We have our usual conversation while Chaia eats. We talk about life in general, how things are going. There's always something on her mind, except boys. She hates boys. (Later this will change drastically. Trust me.)

When I finish eating, Daddy says we are going someplace very special— the Monkey Jungle. It is a park with different kinds of monkeys, including chimpanzees and gorillas. Daddy buys me cotton candy, and we stroll together in the sunshine.

After lunch, I suggest that we go to the Monkey Jungle. We both love this place, which is literally a jungle full of monkeys and parrots.

I spot a large cage with a huge black gorilla with a silver back. I run up to the cage and see that his name is Booloo. I call out to him, and he turns around and charges right at me!

Chaia, being a friendly sort, leans up against the cage and yells "BOOLOO!" Booloo turns around, takes one step toward Chaia, and she runs out of the Monkey Jungle.

I drop the cotton candy and run for my life! Daddy finally catches up with me and hugs me so I won't be afraid. I feel safe with him.

I run fiercely behind her down South Dixie Highway. Needless to say, we do not visit Booloo again.

We head to the movie theater where *Pinocchio* is playing, and we get a perfect seat right in the center. The movie is great. All of a sudden Jiminy Cricket starts to sing "When You Wish Upon a Star," and I jump up and cry, "Daddy! They're playing our song!" I am so happy that the song Daddy and I share has become famous.

Every night before Chaia went to sleep, before the divorce, I would sing her favorite song, "When You Wish Upon a Star." I loved holding her and looking up at the stars and pointing. I would sing the words that Jiminy Cricket is now singing in his wonderful soft-voiced way.

Later we go to Daddy's apartment, and I think how strange it is to see his things so far from home. Mom packed a dress for me that's so blue, it feels like I'm wearing the sky. I am very excited about my first dressy dinner with just me and Daddy.

The waiter comes over in a tuxedo, a napkin over his right arm. I look at Chaia, who's looking at the menu as if she's intently reading it. The waiter says, "What will the young lady be having this evening?"

The waiter's mouth drops open when I ask if they serve Whoppers®.

He pauses and says, "Ma'am, we don't have Whoppers®." Chaia cannot believe this. She gives me that "What is going on in the world?" look.

The waiter says he will check with
the chef, and sure enough, I have a
Whopper® on the prettiest plate I
have ever seen.

*They send a busboy out to get a Whopper® and an order of french fries,
and they put it on a beautiful plate. But that isn't good enough. It has
to be served on paper. That is eating out!*

Daddy and I have a wonderful time talking and laughing, and
I am sad when it is time to leave. He takes me home.

*I drive Chaia home, and that is always the saddest part
of a day with a daughter when you don't live with her.
I kiss Chaia good night and take her up to the door.*

Daddy points up at the stars and begins to sing to me. Then he tells me a prince story, and I tell him how I hope to meet a prince just like him someday. I also tell him that I "wished upon a star" that I won't be divorced one day. He kisses me and says he hopes so, too.

Divorce is never, ever easy and must be very difficult for Chaia. Much more difficult for her, I think, than for her mommy and daddy, because we can go on to other lives.

I wave to my daddy with one hand, and the other is in my
mommy's hand, squeezing with sadness and longing.
I realize that night, before I go to sleep, that I am
lucky to have great parents even if they are apart.
I remember the day I shared with Daddy, and
that memory stays with me always.

I hope Chaia will never have any
really sad days, and that in spite
of the divorce, she will always
know that Daddy's coming.

I know now that divorce can bring good times as well as bad, and that having two parents who love you, even if they don't live together, is the greatest gift of all.